KNOWING G

Our Faithful Friend

Building Intimacy with God

Six Studies for Groups or Individuals with Notes for Leaders

John D. Sloan

Foreword by J. I. Packer

ZondervanPublishingHouse
Grand Rapids, Michigan

A Division of HarperCollins*Publishers*

OUR FAITHFUL FRIEND: *Building Intimacy with God*
Copyright © 1994 by John D. Sloan

Requests for information should be addressed to:
Zondervan Publishing House
Grand Rapids, MI 49530

ISBN 0-310-48301-8

All Scripture quotations, unless otherwise noted, are taken from the Holy Bible: New International Version®. NIV®. (North American Edition). Copyright © 1973, 1978, 1984 by the International Bible Society. All rights reserved.

All rights reserved. No part of this publication may be reproduced, stored in a retrieval system, or transmitted in any form or by any means—electronic, mechanical, photocopy, recording, or any other—except for brief quotations in printed reviews, without the prior permission of the publisher.

Edited by Jack Kuhatschek
Cover design by Mark Veldheer
Cover photograph by John Higginson
Interior design by Mark Veldheer & Art Jacobs

Printed in the United States of America

94 95 96 97 98 99 / ❖ DP / 10 9 8 7 6 5 4 3 2 1

Contents

Foreword

One big difference between our current culture and that of a century ago is that the Victorians saw life in terms of roles, while we see it in terms of relationships. Real life, we say, is a matter of relationships, for roles minimize personal involvement while relationships maximize it.

In saying this, we speak more Christian truth than perhaps we realize. For real life according to the Bible means relating not just to other people but also to the personal God who made us. We live and move and exist in him, and it is both scandalous and impoverishing when we ignore him.

Who is he? The startling truth is that he is a *society*. The Father, Son, and Holy Spirit share with each other an intimate and loving relationship. Yet in the unity of their interpersonal life, they constitute a single divine being. God is they, a society and a team, and they are he, the only God there is.

A mystery? An inexplicable reality? Yes, but a life-giving one. It is our privilege not simply to acknowledge the truth of the Trinity but also to enter into Spirit-sustained relationship with the Father and the Son—a relationship which from one standpoint is *eternal life*, and from another is *knowing God*.

Knowing people involves, first, knowing facts about them and, second, making their acquaintance. How deep our relationship goes depends on how much empathy we have, how many concerns and interests we share, and how much we seek to exalt the one we love. It is the same with knowing God.

The Bible is God's communication to all who hear or read it. Through its varied contents the Triune Lord tells us about himself and calls us to himself. A proper understanding of the Bible will focus at every point on both the information about God and the invitation to know him.

Knowing God Bible Studies are designed to help you achieve this focus. I heartily recommend them. They generate vision, insight, wisdom, and devotion in equal quantities. Use them and you will be blessed.

J. I. Packer

Knowing God Bible Studies

Every Christian desires a deeper, more personal relationship with God. We long to know him better, to feel his presence, and to experience his power in our lives. Jesus himself tells us, "This is eternal life: that they may know you, the only true God, and Jesus Christ, whom you have sent" (John 17:3).

Knowing God Bible Studies can help you build greater intimacy with God. The series explores who God is and how you can know him better. Each guide focuses on a specific attribute of God, such as his love, his faithfulness, or his mercy. The studies are warm and practical and personal—yet they are firmly grounded in Scripture.

The Knowing God series has been field tested in churches across America, representing a wide variety of denominations. This time-intensive process ensures that the guides have solid biblical content, consistent quality, easy-to-use formats, and helpful leader's notes.

Knowing God Bible Studies are designed to be flexible. You can use the guides in any order that is best for you or your group. They are ideal for Sunday-school classes, small groups, one-on-one relationships, or as materials for your quiet times.

Because each guide contains only six studies, you can easily explore more than one attribute of God. In a Sunday-school class, any two guides can be combined for a quarter (twelve weeks), or the entire series can be covered in a year.

Each study deliberately focuses on a limited number of passages, usually only one or two. That allows you to see each passage in its context, avoiding the temptation of prooftexting and the frustration of "Bible hopscotch" (jumping from verse to verse). If you would like to look up additional passages, a Bible concordance will give the most help.

Knowing God Bible Studies help you *discover* what the Bible says rather than simply *telling* you the answers. The questions encourage you to think and to explore options rather than merely to fill in the blanks with one-word answers.

Leader's notes are provided in the back of each guide. They show how to lead a group discussion, provide additional information on questions, and suggest ways to deal with problems that may come up in the discussion. With such helps, someone with little or no experience can lead an effective study.

SUGGESTIONS FOR INDIVIDUAL STUDY

1. Begin each study with prayer. Ask God to help you understand the passage and to apply it to your life.
2. A good modern translation, such as the *New International Version*, the *New American Standard Bible*, or the *New Revised Standard Version*, will give you the most help. Questions in this guide, however, are based on the *New International Version*.
3. Read and reread the passage(s). You must know what the passage says before you can understand what it means and how it applies to you.
4. Write your answers in the space provided in the study guide. This will help you to clearly express your understanding of the passage.

5. Keep a Bible dictionary handy. Use it to look up any unfamiliar words, names, or places.

SUGGESTIONS FOR GROUP STUDY

1. Come to the study prepared. Careful preparation will greatly enrich your time in group discussion.
2. Be willing to join in the discussion. The leader of the group will not be lecturing but will encourage people to discuss what they have learned in the passage. Plan to share what God has taught you in your individual study.
3. Stick to the passage being studied. Base your answers on the verses being discussed rather than on outside authorities such as commentaries or your favorite author or speaker.
4. Try to be sensitive to the other members of the group. Listen attentively when they speak, and be affirming whenever you can. This will encourage more hesitant members of the group to participate.
5. Be careful not to dominate the discussion. By all means participate! But allow others to have equal time.
6. If you are the discussion leader, you will find additional suggestions and helpful ideas in the leader's notes at the back of the guide.

Introducing Our Faithful Friend

We all long for friendships. We yearn for people who will stand by us through sorrows as well as joys. And the older we get, the more we realize how difficult it is to make true friendships that last throughout our lives.

There was a man who lived in the mid-1600s who felt that God was that type of friend to him. And the man described how anyone could make God their closest and best friend in his small book entitled *The Practice of the Presence of God.*

History records almost nothing about this author except that he was born Nicholas Herman in French Lorraine. He had little education. He performed the duties of a footman and a soldier very briefly. Becoming a convert to Christianity at the age of eighteen, he joined the barefooted Carmelites in Paris as a lay brother in 1666. He then served in the kitchen for this group of Christians until he died at the age of eighty. His friends affectionately called him Brother Lawrence.

Those who knew Brother Lawrence testified that everywhere and always he was close to God. Friends of Lawrence heard him humming hymns and greeting others with love in the middle of the clatter of pots and pans during his sun-up to sun-down days in kitchen drudgery.

M. de Chalons, who collected Brother Lawrence's letters, said that Lawrence's calm and trusting attitude made everyone around him yearn for his joy and friendship with God. Whether it was time for church or time for work, Lawrence "found no difference, because he still continued with God, praising and blessing Him with all his might, so that he passed his life in continual joy."

Brother Lawrence talked about the only thing he wanted on earth, which was his friendship with God. He said that instead of feeling that God was only in his life to rule over him, Lawrence felt that God embraced him with all love and mercy and gave him the key to the treasures of heaven. "God converses and delights Himself with me incessantly, and in a thousand and a thousand ways, He treats me in all respects as His favorite."

Brother Lawrence showed how, at any time and in any place, the person who seeks God can find him. Not through years of denial and meditation. And not as some impersonal force—but as Friend.

This guide contains six studies that will help you build a stronger and deeper friendship with God. You will look at the examples of those who knew God intimately—Abraham, Sarah, David, Joshua, Jeremiah, Paul, and the Lord Jesus himself. You will also study God's promises to those seeking his friendship: in Genesis, Joshua, the Psalms, Lamentations, 1 Corinthians, and the Gospel of John.

As you seek to come closer to God, may you discover the astonishing reality of Jesus' words—"You are my friends."

John D. Sloan

1

Longing for Intimacy

Psalm 63

His mom died when he was three, and his dad raised him the best he could, putting him to bed with stories of Babe Ruth, Lou Gehrig, and Shoeless Joe Jackson instead of the rhymes of Mother Goose. But John and Ray Kinsella found they disagreed on just about everything as Ray grew older. So Ray left home and thought he would never look back. To his surprise, the yearning to see his father grew stronger and stronger as the years went by.

As the movie *Field of Dreams* begins, we find out that Ray never got the chance to see his father again. His dad died a few years after Ray left home for college. In one scene Ray's friend, Terrence Mann, asks about John Kinsella.

"What happened to your father?"

"He never made it as a ballplayer, so he tried to get his son to make it for him," says Ray wryly. "By the time I was ten, playing baseball was like eating vegetables or taking out the trash. So when I was fourteen I started to refuse. Think of that. An American boy refusing to have catch with his father.

"When I was seventeen, I packed my things, said something awful, and left. After a while I wanted to come home but I didn't know how. He died before I could take back what I said.

He died before I could tell him I love him. He never met my wife. He never saw his granddaughter." The entire movie is about Ray's longing—Ray's dream—to be with his father once again.

David expresses that same intense longing for his heavenly Father in Psalm 63. Though he was known as "a man after God's own heart," David and his family sinned against the Lord. These sins resulted in David's banishment into the wilderness beyond the royal city of Jerusalem. During that exile, he recorded his heartfelt longing for his friend, God.

---

1. When do you miss your friends most? Explain.

2. Read Psalm 63:1–11. What are some of the feelings David expresses to God about how much he misses his companionship?

3. David compares his longing for God to an unquenchable thirst (v. 1). Why is this a good image for yearning for one you love?

4. To what extent do you share David's deep longing and thirst for God? (Be honest.)

5. David reflects about seeing God in the great place of Israel's worship (v. 2). What are the "glory" and "power" that David remembers longingly?

6. Because of the great price tag David places on his friendship with God, what verbal habit does David vow to practice toward his Friend (vv. 3–5)?

How do our praises and positive affirmations of God strengthen our relationship with him?

7. David's thoughts about God are not limited to a particular time of day or period in life (vv. 4, 6). Why should we give continual attention to our friendship with God?

8. David writes that continually he thought about, sang about, and clung to God (vv. 6-8). What spiritual exercises do you think David did to remember, think about, and cling to God?

9. When you spend time thinking about your friends and then tell them in person you like them, what happens to your feelings about them? Why?

How might these same practices strengthen your feelings about God?

10. David's friendship with God spelled trouble for his enemies (vv. 9–11). Why was David so confident in his eventual victories, even though at this point he was on the run?

11. How do David's emotions at the beginning of the psalm (v. 1) compare to his emotion at the end (v. 11)?

12. Name some of the benefits of David's friendship with God. (For instance, God's protection—vv. 7-9.)

13. What kinds of changes do you need to make in your schedule so you can make more room for friendship with God?

14. Ask God for the desire and the time to make him more of a valued person in your life. Ask him to give you a longing not for success or for winning, but for him.

Memory Verse

O God, you are my God, earnestly I seek you; my soul thirsts for you, my body longs for you, in a dry and weary land where there is no water.

Psalm 63:1

BETWEEN STUDIES

Do what David did. Get a sheet of paper and write down a letter to God that expresses how much you miss him, how important he is to you, and how you want to know of his presence near you all day and all night long. Tell him how much you love him. Write the words "Psalm 1" at the top and middle of the page, with "a psalm of [your name]" underneath. Keep this sheet with you throughout the week and look at it when you're tempted to think your friendship with God isn't real.

2

I Will Be With You

Joshua 1:1–9

The Secret Service, a part of the Treasury Department, employs 4,300 people to protect the president and to safeguard the nation's money supply. In order to give our commander-in-chief constant protection, these agents stick extremely close to him everywhere he goes. When he's walking, when he's riding in his limousine, when he's on vacation at a ski slope or a lake, the Secret Service is there—surrounding him, jogging by his car, skiing or fishing right beside him. If the president goes scuba diving, agents put on masks and tanks and go with him under the water.

Wouldn't it be nice to have someone who would always be with you, protect you, and help you—not out of duty but because you were friends?

Joshua knew God to be just such a Friend as he stood at the border of Canaan, ready to lead the people of Israel into the Promised Land. In the passage that follows, God makes the greatest promise of all: "I will be with you."

1. Sometimes God does not feel close to us. Why?

2. Read Joshua 1:1–9. Why did Joshua become the new leader of the people of Israel in place of Moses? (Cf. vv. 1–2; Deut. 34:1–12.)

How do you think Joshua felt about filling such big shoes?

3. God promised the Israelites a sizable quantity of real estate and an undefeated season on the battlefield (vv. 3–5). What reasons would the Israelites and Joshua have for believing such a rosy scenario?

4. "As I was with Moses, so I will be with you" (v. 5). What would Joshua understand this statement to mean?

5. Why is the promise of God's presence as our friend and ally so important in all that we do?

Is there ever a time we don't want God around? Explain.

6. God made an identical promise to Jacob (Gen. 28:15), Moses, and Joshua (v. 5). As he looked back at the lives of Jacob and Moses, what thoughts do you think were going through Joshua's mind?

7. The Israelis today have tanks, jets, and missiles to give them courage against their enemies. What were Joshua's two main offensive weapons (vv. 7-9)?

8. Joshua had the "Book of the Law" and heard God speak directly. In what ways does God communicate with us today?

9. God tells Joshua to not just read the Bible but to "meditate on it day and night" (v. 8). What does it mean to "meditate"?

Why is meditation essential for understanding and applying the Bible?

10. "Be strong and courageous" is a repeated refrain in verses 6–9. How was this strength and courage an act of faith for Joshua?

11. In verse 9 God reassures Joshua and his people that he will be with them wherever they go (see also v. 5; Heb. 13:5). Do you feel this reassurance from God? Why or why not?

12 Ask God in prayer to become as close to you as your best friend. Meditate on the promises of Joshua 1:1–9 to remind you of the reality of God's nearness to you.

Memory Verse

Have I not commanded you? Be strong and courageous. Do not be terrified; do not be discouraged, for the LORD your God will be with you wherever you go.

Joshua 1:9

BETWEEN STUDIES

God gave Joshua the good advice to "not let this Book of the Law depart from your mouth; meditate on it day and night." This is good advice for everyone who reads the Bible.

Start a Scripture memory plan this week by taking two of the verses from this study's passage—such as verses 5, 7, 8, or 9—and writing them down on index cards. Take them with you wherever you go. Not only will this start to deepen your relationship with God, it will also remind you of the fact that God is always with you as a Friend.

3

You Are My Friends

John 15:9-15

In October of 1988, veteran sky-diver Frank Farnan jumped from a plane at about 13,000 feet above Clewiston, Florida. Eleven other parachutists made the jump to practice building a formation. But at 10,500 feet, something went wrong. One diver fell into Farnan and knocked him unconscious. Farnan's body tumbled out of control and dropped below the formation, gaining downward momentum as it fell faster than the rest of the group and farther away with every second.

Another veteran in the group, Eddie Turner, and two other jumpers put their hands over their heads and pointed their bodies straight downward, becoming human missiles aimed at the body tumbling hundreds of feet below. At 15 seconds until impact with the ground and at an elevation of only 2,500 feet, the three jumpers reached Farnan's body. Turner grabbed a leg, pulled Farnan's rip cord, and the unconscious jumper's chute opened. Turner had only a few seconds to save himself. Turner emerged from the event unhurt, and Farnan ended up with only a few bruises.

Not many will put their life on the line for a friend. Yet according to John 15, Jesus was willing to do even more than that for those he loved.

1. If someone called you his friend, what things could you expect from him?

What things should you expect to do for him?

2. Read John 15:9–15. Jesus tells his disciples, "Remain in my love" (v. 9). What does it mean to remain in Christ's love (vv. 10-11; see also vv. 1–8)?

3. How does Jesus set a high standard of friendship in verses 12–13?

How would his statements take on added meaning after his death on the cross?

4. Give examples of how you can lay down your life for your friends.

5. Why is obedience the true test of our friendship with Jesus (v. 14)?

6. What are some of the commands Jesus asks us to obey?

7. How can we be sure these are the commands of a friend wanting our best rather than a dictator wanting control?

8. In verse 15 Jesus says he won't call his disciples servants any more, but friends. What do you think the disciples of this notoriously famous teacher felt at that moment?

9. What events could have made Jesus feel confident about bringing his disciples into more of the Master's business (v. 15)?

10. Jesus says that friendship means greater intimacy, a sharing with them of all he has learned from his Father. How would this intimacy change the way the disciples looked at life?

11. Jesus has a lot to tell us as friends. In what specific area of your life (your needs, your wants, your attitudes, your family, your life goals, and so on) do you need to know more of what Jesus has learned from his Father? Explain.

12. Think about Jesus' sacrifice for you as a friend. Ask God to show you ways that you can obey him and begin to get a growing understanding of him—not as his servant, but as his friend.

Memory Verse

Greater love has no one than this, that he lay down his life for his friends.

John 15:13

BETWEEN STUDIES

Start off every day this week by imagining your relationship to God as a relationship between a ruler and his lowly servant. Imagine what the servant's role really is: Responding immediately to every trivial request of the ruler; immediate obedience to commands that may put you in danger without a thought for your safety; acceptance of your place in your ruler's life as just a piece of property; and so on. Write the word *servant* on an index card and take it with you to school or work. During the morning hours, take the card out at various times and remind yourself of the servant's role.

Every day at noon, however, take five minutes out of your lunch break to pull the card out, cross out the word *servant*, and write in the word *friend*. At various times in the second half of each day, rejoice in your new relationship to God.

4

Faithful in Trials

Lamentations 3:1–26

When Helen Keller was only eighteen months old, she lost her sight and hearing because of a severe illness. Until the age of six, she was the selfish center of the Keller household, and everything sympathetically revolved around her. Then Anne Sullivan, a twenty-one-year-old graduate of the Perkins Institution for the Blind, arrived in Tuscumbia, Alabama, from Boston. Anne was there to open up Helen's world. But the trials Helen put her teacher through are legendary—the wrestling matches over the utensils Helen refused to use, the tug-of-war battles between Anne and the Keller family over Helen's welfare, and the sneak attacks from the fighting, biting, incorrigible Helen.

But Anne's patience and faithfulness to Helen paid off. Not only did Anne give Helen the gift of language, but she accompanied Helen throughout her entire education, including an exemplary college program in which Anne would read books "into Helen's hand" on many late nights so Helen's course work would not be hindered. Helen Keller became an ambassador for the blind and the deaf and a monument to the heights a human can reach.

In her second autobiography Helen wrote that Anne "was a delightful companion, entering into all my discoveries with the joy of a fellow explorer. . . . Above all she loved me. . . . By the vitalizing power of her friendship she has stirred and enlarged my faculties." The book's dedication reads simply: "To Anne Sullivan, whose love is the story of my life."[1]

Anne Sullivan was faithful to Helen Keller through trials, around obstacles, and over mountains that would have stopped Helen's successful pilgrimage through life. God wants to be our faithful friend through all of our trials. The Book of Lamentations plainly shows how God, the faithful one, is always there for his friends, even in the midst of great trials and suffering.

---

1. When things are not going well in your life, who generally gets the blame? Your spouse? One of your children? A parent? The dog? A friend? Anyone else?

2. Read Lamentations 3:1–20. What is your impression of the writer's view of his circumstances and of God from these verses?

3. What must the writer have been feeling about God to have penned the following phrases: "He has driven me away; he has made my skin and my flesh grow old; he has walled me in so I cannot escape; like a lion hiding, he dragged me from the path and mangled me; he has broken my teeth with gravel"?

4. When we face heartbreaking circumstances, what value is there in talking about our feelings of anger, pain, and frustration?

5. Read verses 21–26. A change of mood occurs in these verses. What could account for the attitude change in the writer?

6. The writer makes an almost incomprehensible statement in verses 22–23, seeing that the city of Jerusalem and the temple lay in ruins and the people were forced into captivity. What would the average Jewish refugee have thought as the writer proclaimed this statement on a burned-out street corner?

How could the writer convince a cynic of God's goodness?

7. The author of Lamentations stresses that we can always count on God's love and faithfulness (vv. 22–23). What does this promise mean to you?

8. Why would God's protective love and the faithfulness the writer has experienced throughout his life make him willing to wait for the Lord (v. 24)?

What would "waiting" mean to the native of Judah who was homeless or deported by invaders?

9. How can the writer's view in verse 24 help you to turn to God even in the middle of painful circumstances?

10. What is called "good" in verses 25 and 26?

How do God's actions and our actions fit together as we view the events of this world?

11. How can our view of God's nearness to us in time of trial change our feelings about what is happening?

How can it change more than just our feelings?

12. Ask God to give you insight and courage to see that he is with you in the midst of every trial. Pray for the wisdom to look first for him.

Memory Verse

Because of the LORD's great love we are not consumed, for his compassions never fail. They are new every morning; great is your faithfulness.

Lamentations 3:22–23

BETWEEN STUDIES

Think back to the last calamity of your life. Did you seek God in the midst of your pain or not? If you didn't, list some of the statements from Lamentations 3:19–26 that could have encouraged you by reminding you God was near. If you did, think of a friend who is going through difficulties and list some of the Lamentations statements that might apply to his or her problem. Then pray that the person might see God in the midst of the trial.

Note

1. Helen Keller, *Midstream: My Later Life* (Garden City, N.Y.: Doubleday, Doran and Co., 1930], 344–46.)

5

Faithful in Temptation

1 Corinthians 10:1-13

In John Bunyan's *Pilgrim's Progress*, a man named Christian is making his way from this world to the next, encountering pitfalls, dangers, and monsters along the way. The Slough of Despond, Apollyon, Vanity Fair, Doubting Castle, and Dark River are just a few of the obstacles that stand in the path of his journey.

For example, as Christian passes by a hill called Lucre, a man named Demas beckons and offers the riches of his silver mine. Christian hurries past, realizing the danger, but others immediately take the invitation of Demas, to their great regret. As they greedily climb up to look into the mine, they lose their footing and fall into the pit where they sink into the depths.

Christian escaped the temptations that swallowed others because he obeyed the words of the Great Book that started his journey. That Book tells us that we, too, can escape temptation because God, our friend, is with us on our journey.

1. Do you think people in our modern culture face greater temptations than previous generations did? Explain.

2. Read 1 Corinthians 10:1–13. Why does Paul give this short history of Israel to the Corinthians (vv. 1–12)?

3. The Israelites were guilty of idolatry, sexual immorality, testing the Lord, and grumbling (vv. 6–10). Why do you think Paul warns the Corinthians against these specific sins?

4. In what ways do Christians today face these same temptations?

What other temptations do we face in today's fast-paced society?

5. Whether it is an experience in childhood that you don't want to repeat or a moral failure that you want to avoid the next time, how can good result from remembering the mistakes of the past?

6. Paul's warning in verse 12 is against the smug confidence some Corinthian believers had about their ability to resist temptations. Why is self-confidence in this area deadly for a Christian?

7. If verse 12 is for the overconfident, then verse 13 is for the despondent and the fearful. How does it help you to know that your temptations are not unique but "common to man"?

8. Although some temptations *seem* unbearable, what assurances does God give us in verse 13?

9. God knows our limits and how much we can bear. When we are tempted, why is it also important for us to know our own limits?

10. God promises to provide us "a way out" of any temptation we face. What are some ways he has helped you to escape temptation?

When you are being tempted, do you consciously look for God's way out? Explain.

11. Think of a recurring temptation that you face. Thank God for being with you in that temptation and for knowing how much you can bear. Ask him to show you the way out of the temptation.

Memory Verse

No temptation has seized you except what is common to man. And God is faithful; he will not let you to be tempted beyond what you can bear. But when you are tempted, he will also provide a way out so that you can stand up under it.

1 Corinthians 10:13

BETWEEN STUDIES

Some of the biggest temptations in any house lurk behind the door of the large, upright appliance that sits in the middle of the kitchen. Write 1 Corinthians 10:13 in a modern translation or paraphrase and stick it on the refrigerator door so that its words greet each visitor. Ask God for help with the temptation of over-snacking this week.

Once you see that God can help in this prominent area, prepare similar renderings of 1 Corinthians 10:13 to be used where temptations meet you daily—at work, in school, at home, or in your entertainment and leisure-time activities.

6

Faithful to His Promises

Genesis 18:1-15
James 2:21-23

Atticus Finch in Harper Lee's classic book *To Kill a Mockingbird* is described by his daughter, Scout, as Maycomb County's best lawyer and a good single father to her and her older brother, Jem. Atticus promised his children he would never give them reason to doubt him or his promises to them as their father.

On the night the children were caught in the middle of hate and racial strife in Maycomb, and Jem's arm was broken at the elbow, Atticus took them back into their home with the warm assurance that everything would again be all right. Scout describes her father's faithfulness beautifully in the closing words of the novel. "Atticus turned out the light and went into Jem's room. He would be there all night, and he would be there when Jem waked up in the morning."[1]

When God promised Abraham and Sarah they would have a son, he did not go back on his word, in spite of the difficulties. As we discover in Genesis 18, God is always faithful to his promises.

1. When someone makes a promise to you, what factors make you believe or disbelieve the promise?

2. Read Genesis 18:1–15. How does Abraham show Near Eastern hospitality to these three special visitors (vv. 1–8)?

3. On three previous occasions the Lord made a promise to Abraham about his descendants (see Gen. 12:2; 15:4–5; 17:1–6). Now the Lord reaffirms his promise. If you were Abraham, how would you have felt about being told at age 75 that you'd have a child (12:4)? At age 99 (17:1)?

4. Sarah laughed when she heard the news of a coming child (v. 12). Abraham had laughed at the news on another occasion (17:17). What do you think the writer of Genesis is emphasizing with these accounts of laughter?

5. Abraham was 99 and Sarah was 89 (17:17). What do you think God's purpose was in stacking up such impossible odds against couple's ability to have a baby?

6. Although the promised birth was humanly impossible, the Lord repeats his promise in verse 10 and verses 13–14. What does this teach you about repeating God's word in the face of apparent failure?

Why does God repeat himself throughout Scripture?

7. How would you have answered this question for our two Bible characters: "Is anything too hard for the LORD?" (v. 14). (Before you give a quick answer, think about the twenty-five years Abraham and Sarah waited for a baby.)

8. What are some other situations in the Bible that seemed "too hard for the LORD" to handle?

9. How does it help you to know that famous people in the Bible faced circumstances they called "too hard for the LORD"?

10. Read James 2:21–23. How would you have felt if God had asked you to put to death the promised son you had waited for all your life?

11. If Abraham had already believed God's promise to provide him an heir (see Gen. 15:6), then why do you think God asked Abraham for Isaac's life?

12. Did God seem like he was going back on his promise to Abraham in asking him to sacrifice Isaac? Explain.

13. Why do you think God called Abraham his friend (v. 23; 2 Chron. 20:7)?

14. How does the story of Abraham and Sarah and Isaac help you understand the character of God and his promises to you?

15. Ask God to help you see that his promises are not just statements in a book but realities he will bring true in your life as you believe.

Memory Verse

And the scripture was fulfilled that says, "Abraham believed God, and it was credited to him as righteousness," and he was called God's friend.

James 2:23

BETWEEN STUDIES

Everyone has experienced at least one disappointment in life—a broken friendship, family or marital problems, career failures, lost opportunities, or countless other situations. Whatever it is, it may seem that God didn't keep his promise to you. Write down one of these situations from your life and pray each morning about it this week. Ask God to lead you to verses that will give you either hope in promises not yet complete or comfort in promises whose fulfillment lies beyond this life. Thank him that he is your friend and you are his.

Note

1. Harper Lee, *To Kill a Mockingbird* (New York: Warner Books, 1960), 281.

Leader's Notes

Leading a Bible discussion—especially for the first time—can make you feel both nervous and excited. If you are nervous, realize that you are in good company. Many biblical leaders, such as Moses, Joshua, and the apostle Paul, felt nervous and inadequate to lead others (see, for example, 1 Cor. 2:3). Yet God's grace was sufficient for them, just as it will be for you.

Some excitement is also natural. Your leadership is a gift to the others in the group. Keep in mind, however, that other group members also share responsibility for the group. Your role is simply to stimulate discussion by asking questions and encouraging people to respond. The suggestions listed below can help you to be an effective leader.

PREPARING TO LEAD

1. Ask God to help you understand and apply the passage to your own life. Unless that happens, you will not be prepared to lead others.
2. Carefully work through each question in the study guide. Meditate and reflect on the passage as you formulate your answers.
3. Familiarize yourself with the leader's notes for the study. These will help you understand the purpose of the study

and will provide valuable information about the questions in the study.

4. Pray for the various members of the group. Ask God to use these studies to make you better disciples of Jesus Christ.
5. Before the first meeting, make sure each person has a study guide. Encourage them to prepare beforehand for each study.

LEADING THE STUDY

1. Begin the study on time. If people realize that the study begins on schedule, they will work harder to arrive on time.
2. At the beginning of your first time together, explain that these studies are designed to be discussions, not lectures. Encourage everyone to participate, but realize that some may be hesitant to speak during the first few sessions.
3. Read the introductory paragraph at the beginning of the discussion. This will orient the group to the passage being studied.
4. Read the passage aloud. You may choose to do this yourself, or you might ask for volunteers.
5. The questions in the guide are designed to be used just as they are written. If you wish, you may simply read each one aloud to the group. Or you may prefer to express them in your own words. Unnecessary rewording of the questions, however, is not recommended.
6. Don't be afraid of silence. People in the group may need time to think before responding.
7. Avoid answering your own questions. If necessary, rephrase a question until it is clearly understood. Even an eager group will quickly become passive and silent if they think the leader will do most of the talking.
8. Encourage more than one answer to each question. Ask, "What do the rest of you think?" or "Anyone else?" until several people have had a chance to respond.

9. Try to be affirming whenever possible. Let people know you appreciate their insights into the passage.
10. Never reject an answer. If it is clearly wrong, ask, "Which verse led you to that conclusion?" Or let the group handle the problem by asking them what they think about the question.
11. Avoid going off on tangents. If people wander off course, gently bring them back to the passage being considered.
12. Conclude your time together with conversational prayer. Ask God to help you apply those things that you learned in the study.
13. End on time. This will be easier if you control the pace of the discussion by not spending too much time on some questions or too little on others.

Many more suggestions and helps are found in the book *Leading Bible Discussions* (InterVarsity Press). Reading it would be well worth your time.

STUDY ONE

Longing for Intimacy

PSALM 63

Purpose: To develop a longing and a desire for intimacy with God.

Question 1 Every study begins with a "warm-up question," which is discussed *before* reading the passage. A warm-up question is designed to do three things.

First, it helps to break the ice. Because a warm-up question doesn't require any knowledge of the passage or any special preparation, it can get people talking and can help them to feel more comfortable with each other.

Second, a warm-up question can motivate people to study the passage at hand. At the beginning of the study, people in the group aren't necessarily ready to jump into the world of the Bible. Their minds may be on other things (their kids, a problem at work, an upcoming meeting) that have nothing to do with the study. A warm-up question can capture their interest and draw them into the discussion by raising important issues related to the study. The question becomes a bridge between their personal lives and the answers found in Scripture.

Third, a good warm-up question can reveal where people's thoughts or feelings need to be transformed by Scripture. That is why it is important to ask the warm-up question *before* reading the passage. The passage might inhibit the spontaneous, honest answers people might have given, because they feel compelled to give biblical answers. The warm-up question allows them to compare their personal thoughts and feelings with what they later discover in Scripture.

Question 2 David wrote this psalm during forced time in the Judean wilderness, most likely during the time of his escape from his son Absalom (2 Sam. 15:13–30). To understand what led up to this un-royal flight of Israel's most noted king, a little history is valuable.

Once David became king over Israel (2 Sam. 5:1–5), he made Jerusalem his royal city and defeated, among other peoples, the Philistines, the Moabites, the warriors of Damascus, the Edomites, and the Ammonites, and thus finished what Joshua had started: to secure the borders of Israel and establish it as the premier nation of God.

Then came David's sin with Bathsheba (2 Sam. 11). His son Amnon sinned against his daughter Tamar (2 Sam. 13). His son Absalom murdered Amnon. Then Absalom led a conspiratorial takeover of his throne (2 Sam. 15). And so David fled out of Jerusalem across the Kidron Valley and into the wilderness (2 Sam. 15:23–28).

Question 3 David's intense longing for God was not just the result of being in the desert. "David's yearning for God was intensified by his keen sense of exclusion from the sanctuary in Jerusalem and his separation form the ark, the symbol of the divine presence (cf. 2 Sam. 15:25, 26)" (Leslie S. M'Caw, "The Psalms," *The New Bible Commentary, Revised*, ed. J. A. Motyer et al. [Grand Rapids: Eerdmans, 1970], 489).

Question 5 Some interpreters see David's response in verse 2 as the response of one who has seen a vision of God—the same direct vision David had of God when he was in the sanctuary in the temple at Jerusalem. This caused David to suddenly break from despondency into great joy. Most, however, would rather see David's joyful response as part of his longing for God and the ability to worship him in the same manner as he did in former days. David wanted the good old days to return, and he yearned for them so strongly that he could almost taste the brightness of God's glory.

Question 6 "The prayerful praise of God awaits an answer. 'Praise' is the response of faith in God's perfections as they relate to his people. He [David] expects the Lord to come through in time by an abundant provision of his needs. . . . Prayer that is confident of the Lord's fidelity to his promises also expresses praise. The Lord is pleased with the 'lips' of men that joyfully emit sounds of praise" (Willem A. VanGemeren, *Psalms*, The Expositor's Bible Commentary, ed. Frank E. Gaebelein [Grand Rapids: Zondervan, 1991], p. 427).

Question 7 This question is a crucial application of desiring intimacy with God. You may want to focus more time on this idea, making a list of the positives that result from continually giving attention to our relationship with God—like David did in the wilderness. Then list the negatives of ignoring fellowship with God—which is part of what put David in the wilderness.

Question 8 Verse 7 talks about David being "in the shadow of your wings." This is an interesting word picture for being in God's protection and under his care. The Hebrew expression for "shadow" meant to protect against oppression, in the way that shade protects from the oppressive sun (Lam. 4:20; Num. 14:9). And the wings symbolized the protective outreach of God's power (Pss. 36:7; 57:1) (*The NIV Study Bible* [Grand Rapids, Mich.: Zondervan, 1985], p. 800).

STUDY TWO

I Will Be With You

JOSHUA 1:1–9

Purpose: To realize that God is always with us and to understand the impact this truth should have on our lives.

Question 2 Moses forfeited his opportunity to go into the Promised Land. God would only let him see it. Numbers

27:12–14 summarizes the sin of Moses against God at the waters of Meribah Kadesh, in the Desert of Zin, where the people had rebelled over the lack of water. God provided water to the people through Moses, but in his anger against the people Moses didn't follow God's instructions—and did it his way (cf. Num. 20:1–12). This brought dishonor to God and his holiness and caused Moses to miss entering the land. The death of Moses caused God to renew his command to the people to enter the land.

Verse 2 is "a central theme of the Pentateuch [the Bible's first five books] (see Genesis 12:1; 50:24; Exodus 3:8; 23:31; Deuteronomy 1:8). Joshua records the fulfillment of this promise of God" (*The NIV Study Bible*, p. 292).

Question 3 "The dimensions of the land promised to Israel vary (compare this text and Genesis 15:18 with Deuteronomy 34:1–4), but these are the farthest limits—conquered and held only by David and Solomon. . . . Joshua was to take all he set out to conquer; wherever he set his foot was his. His victories gave to the 12 tribes most of the central hill country and much of the Negev" (*The NIV Study Bible*, p. 292). The literal fulfillment of verse 4 came in the reigns of Kings Uzziah and Jeroboam as well as in the times of David and Solomon.

Question 6 Joshua had watched the secret of Moses' success lived out in Moses' life. As Joshua thought about God's promise, he knew that the same conditions of success would exist for him. "The conditions for the promise, 'No one will be able to stand up against you,' are stated in vv. 6–9. It was Israel's failure to observe these conditions that caused their humiliating defeat at Ai (Joshua 7:1–5). ". . . The secret of Moses' success had been God's presence with him. It would be the secret of Joshua's success also, and it continues to be the secret of success for the church (cf. Matthew 28:19–20)" (Donald H. Madvig, "Joshua," *The Expositor's Bible Commentary*, ed. Frank E. Gaebelein [Grand Rapids, Mich.: Zondervan, 1992], p. 256).

Question 8 There may be differences of opinion within the group as to how God speaks today. Allow people to freely express their opinions, but focus on how God speaks to us through his Word, which is universally agreed upon by Christians.

Question 9 Have you ever thought that talking to yourself might be good? In the case of Scripture it is. "The phrase 'from your mouth' refers to the custom of muttering while studying or reflecting. The Hebrew word translated 'meditate' (*hagah*) literally means 'mutter'. When one continually mutters God's Word to himself, he is constantly thinking about it" (Donald H. Madvig, "Joshua," *The Expositor's Bible Commentary*, p. 257).

STUDY THREE

You Are My Friends

JOHN 15:9–15

Purpose: To understand what it means to be friends with the Lord.

Question 2 In verses 1–8 Jesus used the imagery of a vine and its branches to illustrate his relationship with his disciples. Merrill C. Tenney writes, "It is possible that if the text of this discourse was spoken as they walked from the upper room in Jerusalem down into the Kidron Valley and across to the Mount of Olives, they could have seen the great golden vine, the national emblem of Israel, on the front of the temple" (*John*, The Expositor's Bible Commentary, ed. Frank E. Gaebelein [Grand Rapids, Mich.: Zondervan, 1981], p. 150).

The properties of the vine make it a good object lesson for Jesus to use. To really be a part of a plant or vine, and be considered as a part of that plant's genuine fruit, one has to be connected to that very vine. Just being a grape doesn't make one the stock from one particular vine; connection to that selected vine is necessary. And all the sustenance that a grape derives it derives from the vine—and the vine only. So to really be part of Jesus' life requires intimate connection with him. And all needs will be supplied by him. Obedience to Christ's commands (v. 11) is the true test of whether we remain in his love.

Question 3 At some point in the discussion, have the group turn to 1 John 3:16, a passage that shows that whatever John originally thought about Jesus' words, he caught the full meaning after the Lord's death. "This is how we know what love is: Jesus Christ laid down his life for us. And we ought to lay down our lives for our brothers."

Question 5 Those who want to be considered Jesus' friends must demonstrate their friendship through obedience. Yet this obedience is far different from the old religious system of rules and rituals that Jesus dismantled through his preaching. Now obedience has a whole new motivation in sight: "Faith must be linked with love which will lead to obedience. 'My commandments' (John 14:15) refers to all the content of the Lord's teaching. This principle of observance of commandments through the motive of love is a revolutionary advance over the Jewish approach to the Mosaic law" (Donald Guthrie, "John," *The New Bible Commentary*, p. 958).

Question 8 Contrast the concepts of servant and friend in the group. Make note of differences such as unquestioning obedience with no knowledge of a master's plan as compared to the voluntary service from one who is a confidant.

Question 10 The disciples believed that God and Jesus knew all about their lives (as evidenced by the way Jesus talked about their pasts when he recruited them). Now, however, Jesus was saying that through him the disciples would know the mind of God and his plans. One conclusion the disciples would come to was that this arrangement would not only assure them that they were doing the right things but that God would bring these things to a successful conclusion.

STUDY FOUR

Faithful in Trials

LAMENTATIONS 3:1–26

Purpose: To show that God is a faithful friend to Christians, even in the midst of suffering.

Question 2 In the original Hebrew Bible, the book of Lamentations is anonymous as to authorship. But tradition holds that the prophet Jeremiah—or possibly one of his younger contemporaries—wrote the book of Lamentations as an eyewitness response to the calamities that fell on Jerusalem when Babylonian armies overran her in 587–586 B.C. Some of the material in the five laments (or five chapters) is on a national scale, in which Jeremiah cries out for the nation, while some of it is on a personal scale, such as the material in chapter 3.

With this setting, then, one can see that the first part of chapter 3 dwells on the ills the writer and his nation have suffered. "This chapter . . . concentrates on the personal sufferings of the writer, although he is speaking, no doubt, 'as the typical representative of his people' (T. H. Gaster)" (L. E. H. Stephens-Hodge, "Lamentations," *The New Bible Commentary*, p. 662). The writer attributes the bad times to God.

Question 5 Throughout this book the writer reflects on the responsibility of the ills that have come to him and his nation, and he has concluded here and elsewhere that it is not God's fault or even that of the invaders, but an event the people have brought upon themselves. "The author of Lamentations understands clearly that the Babylonians were merely the human agents of divine retribution and that God himself has destroyed his city and the temple (1:12–15; 2:1–8, 17, 22; 4:11). Nor was the Lord's action arbitrary; blatant, God-defying sin and covenant-breaking rebellion were the root causes of his people's woes (1:5, 8–9; 4:13; 5:7, 16)" (*The NIV Study Bible*, p. 1216).

Question 6 "The vital word in this verse is *hesed* ('great love'), the covenant love and loyalty of the Lord that leads to . . . 'compassion' or 'mercy.' . . . The covenant had called Israel into existence, and the Lord's loving mercy to what he had created would not end" (H. L. Ellison, "Lamentations," *The Expositor's Bible Commentary*, ed. Frank E. Gaebelein [Grand Rapids, Mich.: Zondervan, 1986], p. 720).

Question 10 "The significance of this word [*good*] in Hebrew may escape the modern reader. For us it tends to mean that which conforms to our concepts, but in the OT it is above all that which expresses God's will and purpose. Here there is the acceptance of God's time and God's will (v. 25), faith expressing itself in quiet hope and the learning of discipline (v. 26)" (Ellison, "Lamentations," p. 720).

Question 11 "In the middle of the book, the theology of Lamentations reaches its apex as it focuses on the goodness of

God. He is the Lord of hope (3:21, 24–25), of love (3:22), of faithfulness (3:23), of salvation (3:26). In spite of all evidence to the contrary, 'his compassions never fail. They are new every morning; great is your faithfulness' (3:22–23)" (*The NIV Study Bible*, p. 1216).

STUDY FIVE

Faithful in Temptation

1 CORINTHIANS 10:1–13

Purpose: To realize that we can overcome any temptation we face because God, our friend, is with us.

Question 2 "In this passage Paul takes the sins of Israel during the time of Moses as a basis for warning the Corinthians. Though the people of Israel had the covenant blessings and were miraculously delivered and sustained, yet most of them died in the wilderness because of disobedience and unbelief. Paul uses their experiences as examples, which he exhorts the Corinthians to heed" (W. Harold Mare, "1 Corinthians," *The Expositor's Bible Commentary*, ed. Frank E. Gaebelein [Grand Rapids: Zondervan, 1976], p. 248).

Question 3 Corinth was an important, wealthy city, with an array of distractions that would easily be described as living in the fast lane. "Proximity to the seas and its nearness to Athens, only forty-five miles to the northeast, gave Corinth a position of strategic commercial importance and military defense. . . . The city received shipping from Italy, Sicily, and Spain, as well as from Asia Minor, Syria, Phoenicia, and Egypt. . . . During the Roman period and in its position as a political center, Corinth again became prosperous, with vast income coming from its sea trade and from the development of its arts and industries. . . . The celebration of the Isthmian games at the temple of Poseidon made a considerable contribution to Hellenic life. . . . But with the games there came an emphasis on luxury and profligacy, because the sanctuary of Poseidon was given over to the worship of the Corinthian Aphrodite (probably a counterpart of the Syrian Astarte), whose temple on the Acrocorinth had more than 1,000 *hierodouloi* (female prostitutes). Strabo says that many people came to Corinth on account of these priestesses" (Mare, "1 Corinthians," pp. 175–76).

It is obvious from the entire drift of this letter that things weren't going well in the Corinthian church, and someone had communicated that to Paul. Not only were the Corinthians having a problem in understanding the proper use of the freedoms they had in Christ (chs. 8–10), which had made them vulnerable to a lot of temptations they should have avoided, but they practiced immorality (ch. 5), entered into litigation against other believers (ch. 6), displayed improper conduct during the Lord's Supper and worship (chs. 11, 14), and they had developed false views of the resurrection of Christ (ch. 15).

Questions 7–8 "Verse 13 is one of the most helpful verses in the New Testament and presents the great antidote to falling into sin through temptation" (Mare, "1 Corinthians," 250).

Question 10 "Provide (lit. 'make') the way of escape. The Greek suggests an army trapped in the mountains slipping out though a narrow pass" (Donald Guthrie, "1 Corinthians," *The New Bible Commentary*, p. 1064).

STUDY SIX

Faithful to His Promises

GENESIS 18:1–15; JAMES 2:21–23

Purpose: To discover from the examples of Abraham and Sarah that God is always faithful to his promises.

Question 2 Who were these visitors? According to *The NIV Study Bible*, "At least two of the 'men' were angels (see 19:1; see also note on 16:7). The third may have been the Lord himself (see vv. 1, 13, 17, 20, 26, 33; see especially v. 22)" (p. 32). The last visit from an angel of the Lord occurred in Genesis 16:7, where an angel of the Lord visited Hagar in the desert in her time of need.

John H. Sailhamer believes that all three men represented the Lord: "Though God himself did not appear to Abraham in physical form, the three men are to be seen as representative of his presence. In much the same way the Burning Bush of Exodus 3:2–3 was a physical representation of God's presence but yet was not actually the physical presence of God. In such a way the actual presence of God among his covenant people was assured but without leaving the impression that God may have a physical form" ("Genesis," *The Expositor's Bible Commentary*

[Grand Rapids, Mich.: Zondervan, 1990], p. 145). In any event, the message to Abraham and Sarah was directly from God.

Question 3 Both Sarah and Abraham had previously shown their strong disbelief about God's ability to keep his promise of providing an heir to such an elderly couple. Thirteen years before, Sarah had concocted a scheme to help God out by giving her handmaiden Hagar to Abraham as a surrogate son-bearer (cf. 16:15, 16). The plan to assist God in the face of their impossible ages backfired on a number of fronts, most of all in Sarah and Abraham's relationship. And God's agreement, his covenant, would ultimately be with the naturally born offspring. "Legally, a natural son, even though born after the son of a slave-wife, became the chief heir" (Meredith G. Kline, "Genesis," *The New Bible Commentary*, p. 97).

Question 4 These narratives about Abraham and Sarah are full of the "Name Game" and show God's sense of humor. "Isaac" literally means "he laughs," and readers of Scripture can tell by Abraham's and Sarah's response why God chose the boy's name. But it doesn't end there. "The names of Abram and Sarai are changed [to Abraham and Sarah] by adding the same sound, 'ah-ah,' as though God were laughing with the parents-to-be! Combining a pun with his promise, he put laughter into their very names: the union of aged Abraham and Sarah will produce Laughter-Isaac" (Kline, "Genesis," p. 97).

Question 5 "The point of the verses is that they bring the promise to the brink of failure, pushing the obstacle to its fulfillment far beyond the previous levels. It was not only that Sarah was barren (11:30; 16:1) or that Abraham was old (since he later had children without any apparent divine intervention, 25:1–4). These obstacles in themselves are great enough to demonstrate that the promise, when fulfilled, came from God alone. But the author takes the reader one step further. Sarah was even past the physical age of bearing children. For her to have a child was not simply unlikely; it was impossible" (Sailhamer, "Genesis," pp. 147–48).

Question 7 A few other passages you might want to consider as you answer this question include: Jeremiah 32:17–23, 26–27, a narrative that includes everything from the miracle of creation to God's supernatural deliverance of Israel from Egypt; Luke

1:34–37, the account of an incredible birth to a virgin mother; and Matthew 19:25–26, the declaration of the improbable and impossible salvation of humanity. Kline says it well: "His infinite wisdom makes the laughable believable" (Kline, "Genesis," p. 97).

NOTES

NOTES

NOTES